Simple & Delicious

CHRISTMAS

Simple & Delicious
CHRISTMAS

OVER 100 SENSATIONAL RECIPES FOR THE CHRISTMAS SEASON

This edition published in 2012
LOVE FOOD is an imprint of Parragon Books Ltd

Parragon
Queen Street House
4 Queen Street
Bath BA1 1HE, UK

www.parragon.com/lovefood

ISBN: 978-1-4454-8264-4

Printed in China

Cover Design by Geoff Borin
Photography by Clive Bozzard-HIll
Home Economy by Valerie Barret and Carol Tennant

Notes for the Reader
This book uses both metric and imperial measurements. Follow the same units of measurement throughout; do not mix metric and imperial. All spoon measurements are level: teaspoons are assumed to be 5 ml, and tablespoons are assumed to be 15 ml. Unless otherwise stated, milk is assumed to be full fat, eggs and individual vegetables are medium, and pepper is freshly ground black pepper. Unless otherwise stated, all root vegetables should be washed and peeled prior to using.

Garnishes, decorations and serving suggestions are all optional and not necessarily included in the recipe ingredients or method.

The times given are an approximate guide only. Preparation times differ according to the techniques used by different people and the cooking times may also vary from those given. Optional ingredients, variations or serving suggestions have not been included in the time calculations.

Recipes using raw or very lightly cooked eggs should be avoided by infants, the elderly, pregnant women, convalescents and anyone suffering from an illness. Pregnant and breastfeeding women are advised to avoid eating peanuts and peanut products. Sufferers from nut allergies should be aware that some of the ready-made ingredients used in the recipes in this book may contain nuts. Always check the packaging before use.

Contents

Introduction

The thought of entertaining over the festive period can be quite daunting for many people and if the idea fills you with dread, then help is at hand. This cookbook is here to guide you all the way and features many of the traditional Christmas recipes made easy, plus lots of additional tasty ideas to tempt your taste buds.

Careful planning and organizing

With a bit of careful planning and organizing, the time and effort spent on preparing a traditional Christmas dinner can be reduced, allowing you to relax and enjoy more time with your guests. After all, sharing good food and wine with your family and close friends is one of the real bonuses of Christmas.

Taking the stress out of Christmas

Removing some of the pressures of Christmas will help to ensure a successful and enjoyable event on the day. The best way to cope with feeding a group over the Christmas festivities is to be prepared and organized and to think well ahead. Make lists, lists and more lists! Shopping lists are vital and lists of things to do and when to do them will prove to be very useful.

Traditional Christmas dinner time planner

Sit down and work out how to plan your time for the big day, starting from when you put the turkey into the oven right up to the time you are planning to serve the meal.

The best way to compile a time planner is to work backwards from the time that you want to serve the meal, and write down key timings, for example, what time the turkey needs to go in the oven (remember to preheat the oven beforehand!), when the Christmas pudding should go on to steam, what to do about the stuffing, roast potatoes and parsnips and when the bread sauce and cranberry sauce should be prepared. If you have everything written down in front of you it is so much easier to follow and you will know what you have to do and when.

Even if you are not serving the traditional Christmas dinner, a time planner for your Christmas day meal will be very helpful. There will be inevitable interruptions, but hopefully a time plan for the day will help to avoid many of those last-minute panics. Remember too to make any notes as you go along as these will be invaluable for the next time round.

Advance preparations

There are several things you can do beforehand to save time on Christmas Day and ensure that everything runs as smoothly as possible. Some dishes can be part or fully prepared in advance, either a day or so before Christmas Day and kept refrigerated, or a few weeks in advance and kept in the freezer (or stored, well-wrapped, in a cool, dry place in the case of the Christmas pudding and cake).

The Christmas pudding and Christmas cake are best made 6–8 weeks or so in advance to allow time for their flavours to develop and mature, so very little preparation is needed for these recipes on the actual day. The Christmas cake will need decorating and this can be done at least a week in advance. If you are making your own mincemeat, it should also be made in advance as it needs time to mature before you use it.

Recipes such as mince pies, stuffings, soups and brandy or rum butter can be made a month or so in advance of the day and frozen until needed. Alternatively, if you prefer, dishes such as stuffings, other accompaniments and mince pies can be made on Christmas Eve. And don't forget, if you have a little spare time to rustle up some tasty chocolate truffles 2 or 3 days beforehand, these will create the perfect end to a perfect meal.

Countdown to Christmas

It is advisable to order your turkey in plenty of time (usually about 4–6 weeks in advance, depending on your supplier), to make sure that you get what you want. In addition, you may also decide to cook a joint of ham or gammon over the festive period and this too is worth ordering beforehand.

A week or so before Christmas do the bulk of your shopping, leaving the fresh foods such as fruit, vegetables, sausages, bread, milk, etc, until a day or so before Christmas Day (preferably on Christmas Eve if you can), to ensure you get the freshest produce possible, as it will need to last over the whole holiday period.

On Christmas Eve, do as many of the final preparations as you can. For example, make the stock for the gravy, prepare as many of the vegetables as possible, make the stuffing(s), lay the table, sort out the drinks and chill the wine (if you have room in your fridge at this stage!) and so on.

Above all, remember that once the Christmas dinner is over and your contented guests are snoozing in their chairs, although you may be feeling a little frazzled and a bit weary, you will now have lots of leftovers and no more cooking to do for a while, so you can relax, put your feet up and enjoy a well-deserved and very merry Christmas!

1

Starters & Snacks

Creamy Carrot & Parsnip Soup

serves 4

4 tbsp butter

1 large onion, chopped

450 g/1 lb carrots, chopped

2 large parsnips, chopped

1 tbsp grated fresh root ginger

1 tsp grated orange rind

600 ml/1 pint vegetable stock

125 ml/4 fl oz single cream

salt and pepper

sprigs of fresh coriander, to garnish

Melt the butter in a large saucepan over a low heat. Add the onion and cook, stirring, for 3 minutes, until slightly softened. Add the carrots and parsnips, cover the pan and cook, stirring occasionally, for about 15 minutes, until the vegetables have softened a little. Stir in the ginger, orange rind and stock. Bring to the boil, then reduce the heat, cover the pan and simmer for 30–35 minutes, until the vegetables are tender. Remove from the heat and leave to cool for 10 minutes.

Transfer the soup to a food processor or blender and process until smooth. Return the soup to the rinsed-out saucepan, stir in the cream and season well with salt and pepper. Warm through gently over a low heat.

Remove from the heat and ladle into soup bowls. Garnish each bowl with pepper and a sprig of coriander and serve.

Wild Mushroom & Sherry Soup

serves 4

2 tbsp olive oil

1 onion, chopped

1 garlic clove, chopped

125 g/4½ oz sweet potato, peeled and chopped

1 leek, trimmed and sliced

200 g/7 oz button and chestnut mushrooms

150 g/5½ oz mixed wild mushrooms

600 ml/1 pint vegetable stock

350 ml/12 fl oz single cream

4 tbsp dry sherry

salt and pepper

Parmesan cheese shavings and sautéed wild mushrooms, to garnish

Heat the oil in a saucepan over a medium heat. Add the onion and garlic and cook, stirring, for 3 minutes, until slightly softened. Add the sweet potato and cook, stirring, for 3 minutes. Add the leek and cook, stirring, for 2 minutes.

Stir in the mushrooms, stock and cream. Bring to the boil, then reduce the heat and simmer gently, stirring occasionally, for 25 minutes. Remove from the heat, stir in the sherry and leave to cool slightly.

Transfer half the soup to a food processor and blend until smooth. Return the mixture to the saucepan with the rest of the soup, season to taste with salt and pepper and reheat gently, stirring. Pour into 4 warmed soup bowls and garnish with Parmesan cheese shavings and sautéed wild mushrooms.

Spiced Pumpkin Soup

serves 4

2 tbsp olive oil

1 onion, chopped

1 garlic clove, chopped

1 tbsp chopped fresh root ginger

1 small red chilli, deseeded and finely chopped

2 tbsp chopped fresh coriander

1 bay leaf

1 kg/2 lb 4 oz pumpkin, peeled, deseeded and diced

600 ml/1 pint vegetable stock

salt and pepper

single cream, to garnish

Heat the oil in a saucepan over a medium heat. Add the onion and garlic and cook, stirring, for 4 minutes, until slightly softened. Add the ginger, chilli, coriander, bay leaf and pumpkin and cook, stirring, for 3 minutes.

Pour in the stock and bring to the boil. Using a slotted spoon, skim any scum from the surface. Reduce the heat and simmer gently, stirring occasionally, for 25 minutes, or until the pumpkin is tender. Remove from the heat, take out and discard the bay leaf and leave to cool slightly.

Transfer the soup to a food processor and blend until smooth (you may have to do this in batches). Return the mixture to the saucepan and season to taste with salt and pepper. Reheat gently, stirring. Remove from the heat, pour into 4 warmed soup bowls, garnish each one with a swirl of cream and serve.

Festive Prawn Cocktail

serves 8

125 ml/4 fl oz tomato ketchup

1 tsp chilli sauce

1 tsp Worcestershire sauce

1 kg/2 lb 4 oz cooked tiger prawns

2 ruby grapefruits

lettuce leaves, shredded

2 avocados, peeled, stoned and diced

mayonnaise

2 large egg yolks

1 tsp English mustard powder

1 tsp salt

300 ml/10 fl oz groundnut oil

1 tsp white wine vinegar

pepper

lime slices and fresh dill sprigs, to garnish

First make the mayonnaise. Put the egg yolks in a bowl, add the mustard powder, pepper to taste and salt and beat together well. Pour the oil into a jug and make sure that your bowl is secure on the work surface by sitting it on a damp cloth. Using an electric or hand whisk, begin to whisk the egg yolks, adding just 1 drop of the oil. Make sure that this has been thoroughly absorbed before adding another drop and whisking well.

Continue adding the oil 1 drop at a time until the mixture thickens and stiffens – at this point, whisk in the vinegar and then continue to dribble in the remaining oil very slowly in a thin stream, whisking constantly, until you have used up all the oil and you have a thick mayonnaise.

Mix the mayonnaise, tomato ketchup, chilli sauce and Worcestershire sauce together in a small bowl. Cover with clingfilm and refrigerate until required.

Remove the heads from the prawns and peel off the shells, leaving the tails intact. Slit along the length of the back of each prawn with a sharp knife and remove and discard the dark vein. Cut off a slice from the top and bottom of each grapefruit, then peel off the skin and all the white pith. Cut between the membranes to separate the segments.

When ready to serve, make a bed of shredded lettuce in the bases of 8 glass dishes. Divide the prawns, grapefruit segments and avocados between them and spoon over the mayonnaise dressing. Serve the cocktails garnished with lime slices and dill sprigs.

Blinis with Prawns & Wasabi Cream

serves 6

350 g/12 oz plain flour

125 g/4½ oz buckwheat flour

2 tsp easy-blend dried yeast

600 ml/1 pint full-fat milk, warmed

6 eggs, separated

3 tbsp unsalted butter, melted

5 tbsp soured cream

50 g/1¾ oz clarified butter

wasabi cream

200 ml/7 fl oz soured cream or crème fraîche

½ tsp wasabi paste, or to taste

salt

to serve

300 g/10½ oz cooked prawns, peeled and deveined

50 g/1¾ oz pickled ginger, thinly sliced

2 tbsp fresh coriander leaves

Sift the flours together into a large bowl and stir in the yeast. Make a hollow in the centre and add the milk, then gradually beat in the flour until you have a smooth batter. Cover and chill in the refrigerator overnight.

Two hours before you need the blinis, remove the bowl from the refrigerator and leave the batter for 1 hour 20 minutes to return to room temperature. Beat in the egg yolks, melted butter and soured cream. In a separate bowl, whisk the egg whites until stiff, then gradually fold into the batter. Cover and leave to rest for 30 minutes.

Meanwhile, make the wasabi cream. Mix the soured cream and wasabi paste together in a small bowl until completely combined. Taste and add a little more wasabi paste if you like it hotter. Season to taste with salt, cover and chill in the refrigerator.

To cook the blinis, heat a little of the clarified butter in a non-stick frying pan over a medium–high heat. When hot and sizzling, drop in 3–4 tablespoonfuls of the batter, spaced well apart, and cook until puffed up and tiny bubbles appear around the edges. Flip them over and cook for a few more minutes on the other side. Remove from the pan and keep warm while you cook the remaining batter.

To serve, spoon a little of the wasabi cream on to a blini, add 1 or 2 prawns and a little ginger, then scatter with a few coriander leaves.

Chestnut, Madeira & Mushroom Tarts

makes 12

pastry

100 g/3½ oz unsalted butter, chilled and diced, plus extra for greasing

225 g/8 oz plain flour, plus extra for dusting

pinch of salt

filling

25 g/1 oz unsalted butter

1 tsp olive oil

1 shallot, finely chopped

1 garlic clove, crushed

8 cooked chestnuts, peeled and roughly chopped

200 g/7 oz chestnut mushrooms, chopped

2 tbsp Madeira

150 ml/5 fl oz double cream

1 egg, plus 1 egg yolk

salt and pepper

chopped fresh parsley, to serve

Lightly grease a 7.5-cm/3-inch, 12-hole muffin tin with butter. Sift the flour into a large bowl, add the salt and rub in the remaining butter until the mixture resembles breadcrumbs. Add a little cold water – just enough to bring the dough together. Knead the dough briefly on a floured work surface.

Divide the pastry in half. Roll out 1 piece of pastry and, using a 9-cm/3½-inch plain pastry cutter, cut out 6 rounds, then roll each round into a 12-cm/4½-inch round. Repeat with the remaining pastry until you have 12 rounds of pastry, then use to line the muffin tin. Chill in the refrigerator for 30 minutes.

Meanwhile, preheat the oven to 200°C/400°F/Gas Mark 6 and make the filling. Melt the butter with the oil in a small frying pan over a low heat, add the shallot and garlic and cook, stirring occasionally, for 5–8 minutes until the shallot is transparent and soft. Add the chestnuts and mushrooms and cook, stirring, for 2 minutes, then add the Madeira and simmer for 2 minutes.

Line the pastry cases with baking paper and fill with baking beans, then bake in the preheated oven for 10 minutes. Carefully lift out the paper and beans, and reduce the oven temperature to 190°C/375°F/Gas Mark 5. Stir the cream, whole egg and egg yolk into the mushroom mixture and season well with salt and pepper. Divide between the pastry cases and bake for 10 minutes. Leave to cool in the tin for 5 minutes, then carefully remove from the tin, scatter with chopped parsley and serve.

Leek & Bacon Tartlets

makes 12

pastry

25 g/1 oz unsalted butter

225 g/8 oz plain flour

pinch of salt

1/2 tsp paprika

100 g/3 1/2 oz unsalted
butter, chilled and diced,
plus extra for greasing

filling

1 tsp olive oil

1 leek, trimmed and
chopped

8 unsmoked streaky bacon
rashers, cut into lardons

2 eggs, beaten

150 ml/5 fl oz double cream

1 tsp snipped fresh chives

salt and pepper

Lightly grease a 7.5-cm/3-inch, 12-hole muffin tin with butter. Sift the flour, salt and paprika into a bowl and rub in the remaining butter until the mixture resembles breadcrumbs. Add a little cold water – just enough to bring the dough together. Knead the dough briefly on a floured work surface.

Divide the pastry in half. Roll out 1 piece of pastry and, using a 9-cm/3 1/2-inch plain cutter, cut out 6 rounds, then roll each round into a 12-cm/4 1/2-inch round. Repeat with the other half of the pastry until you have 12 rounds, then use to line the muffin tin. Cover and chill in the refrigerator for 30 minutes.

Meanwhile, preheat the oven to 200°C/400°F/Gas Mark 6. To make the filling, melt the butter with the oil in a non-stick frying pan over a medium heat, add the leek and cook, stirring frequently, for 5 minutes until soft. Remove with a slotted spoon and set aside. Add the lardons to the frying pan and cook for 5 minutes, or until crisp. Remove and drain on kitchen paper.

Line the pastry cases with baking paper and baking beans and bake in the preheated oven for 10 minutes. Whisk the eggs and cream together in a bowl, season to taste with salt and pepper, then stir in the chives with the cooked leek and bacon. Remove the pastry cases from the oven and carefully lift out the paper and beans. Divide the bacon and leek mixture between the pastry cases and bake for 10 minutes until the tarts are golden and risen. Leave to cool in the tin for 5 minutes, then carefully transfer to a wire rack. Serve warm or cold.

Double Cheese Soufflés

makes 6

25 g/1 oz butter, plus extra for greasing

2 tbsp finely grated Parmesan cheese

175 ml/6 fl oz milk

25 g/1 oz self-raising flour

whole nutmeg, for grating

100 g/3½ oz soft goat's cheese

70 g/2½ oz mature Cheddar cheese, grated

2 large eggs, separated

salt and pepper

Preheat the oven to 200°C/400°F/Gas Mark 6. Put a baking sheet in the oven to warm. Generously grease the inside of 6 small ramekins with butter, add half the Parmesan cheese and shake to coat the butter.

Warm the milk in a small saucepan. Melt the remaining butter in a separate saucepan over a medium heat. Add the flour, stir well to combine and cook, stirring, for 2 minutes until smooth. Add a little of the warmed milk and stir until absorbed. Continue to add the milk a little at a time, stirring constantly, until you have a rich, smooth sauce. Season to taste with salt and pepper, and grate in a little nutmeg. Add the cheeses to the sauce and stir until well combined and melted.

Remove from the heat and leave the sauce to cool a little, then add the egg yolks and stir to combine. In a separate bowl, whisk the egg whites until stiff. Fold a tablespoonful of the egg whites into the cheese sauce, then gradually fold in the remaining egg whites. Spoon into the prepared ramekins and scatter over the remaining Parmesan cheese.

Place the ramekins on the hot baking sheet and bake in the preheated oven for 15 minutes until puffed up and brown. Remove from the oven and serve immediately. The soufflés will collapse quite quickly when taken from the oven, so have your serving plates ready to take the soufflés to the table.

Chicken Liver Pâté

serves 4–6

200 g/7 oz butter

225 g/8 oz trimmed chicken livers, thawed if frozen

2 tbsp Marsala wine or brandy

1½ tsp chopped fresh sage

1 garlic clove, roughly chopped

150 ml/5 fl oz double cream

salt and pepper

fresh bay leaves or sage leaves, to garnish

Melba toast, to serve

Melt 40 g/1½ oz of the butter in a large, heavy-based frying pan. Add the chicken livers and cook over a medium heat for 4 minutes on each side. They should be browned on the outside but still pink in the centre. Transfer to a food processor and process until finely chopped.

Add the Marsala to the frying pan and stir, scraping up any sediment with a wooden spoon, then add to the food processor with the chopped sage, garlic and 100 g/3½ oz of the remaining butter. Process until smooth. Add the cream, season to taste with salt and pepper and process until thoroughly combined and smooth. Spoon the pâté into a dish or individual ramekins, smooth the surface and leave to cool completely.

Melt the remaining butter in a small saucepan, then spoon it over the surface of the pâté, leaving any sediment in the saucepan. Decorate with herb leaves, leave to cool, then cover and chill in the refrigerator. Serve with Melba toast.

Mozzarella Crostini with Pesto & Caviar

serves 4

8 slices white bread, crusts removed

3 tbsp olive oil

200 g/7 oz firm mozzarella cheese, diced

6 tbsp lumpfish roe

pesto

75 g/2¾ oz fresh basil, finely chopped

35 g/1¼ oz pine kernels, finely chopped

2 garlic cloves, finely chopped

3 tbsp olive oil

Preheat the oven to 180°C/350°F/Gas Mark 4. Using a sharp knife, cut the bread into fancy shapes, such as half-moons, stars and Christmas trees. Drizzle with the oil, transfer to an ovenproof dish and bake in the preheated oven for 15 minutes.

While the bread is baking, make the pesto. Put the basil, pine kernels and garlic in a small bowl. Pour in the oil and stir well.

Remove the bread shapes from the oven and leave to cool. Spread a layer of pesto on the shapes, top each one with a piece of mozzarella and some lumpfish roe and serve.

Roast Squash with Cranberries

serves 4

4 acorn or 2 small butternut squash

1 tbsp olive oil, plus extra for oiling

100 g/3½ oz basmati rice

50 g/1¾ oz wild rice

25 g/1 oz butter

1 red onion, thinly sliced

2 garlic cloves, crushed

100 g/3½ oz dried cranberries

50 g/1¾ oz pine kernels, toasted

2 tbsp fresh parsley, finely chopped

whole nutmeg, for grating

70 g/2½ oz fresh white or wholemeal breadcrumbs

25 g/1 oz Parmesan cheese, finely grated

butter, for dotting

salt and pepper

If using acorn squash, cut through the centre and trim the stalk and root so that the squash will stand upright securely, then scoop out and discard the seeds. If using butternut squash, cut lengthways in half and scoop out and discard the seeds. Place the prepared squash on an oiled baking sheet.

Cook the two types of rice separately according to the packet instructions and drain well.

Meanwhile, preheat the oven to 190°C/375°F/Gas Mark 5. Melt the butter with the oil in a frying pan over a medium heat, add the onion and garlic and cook, stirring frequently, for 8 minutes, or until transparent and soft.

Tip all the cooked rice and the cooked onion and garlic into a bowl. Add the cranberries, pine kernels and parsley, grate in a little nutmeg and season to taste with salt and pepper. Mix together well.

Carefully divide the stuffing mixture between the squash, then top with the breadcrumbs and Parmesan cheese and dot with butter. Bake in the preheated oven for 50 minutes, then serve hot.

Smoked Turkey & Stuffing Parcels

makes 12

12 slices smoked turkey breast

4 tbsp cranberry sauce or jelly

400 g/14 oz cooked and cooled sausage-meat stuffing

24 sheets filo pastry, thawed if frozen

70 g/2½ oz butter, melted

Preheat the oven to 190°C/375°F/Gas Mark 5. Put a non-stick baking sheet into the oven to heat.

For each parcel, spread a slice of smoked turkey with a teaspoonful of cranberry sauce, spoon 35 g/1¼ oz of the stuffing into the centre and roll up the turkey slice. Lay 1 sheet of filo pastry on a work surface and brush with a little of the melted butter. Put another sheet on top, then put the rolled-up turkey in the centre. Add a little more cranberry sauce, then carefully fold the filo pastry around the turkey, tucking under the ends to form a neat parcel. Repeat to make 12 parcels.

Place the parcels on the hot baking sheet, brush with the remaining melted butter and bake in the preheated oven for 25 minutes until golden. Serve hot.

Devilled Turkey Legs

serves 4

2 turkey legs, skinned

½ tsp cayenne pepper

2 tbsp Dijon or hot mustard

40 g/1½ oz unsalted butter, softened

salt and pepper

Make deep criss-cross slashes in the turkey legs. Season with salt and pepper and sprinkle with a little of the cayenne pepper. Spread the mustard all over the legs, pressing it well into the slashes. Place the legs in a large, deep dish, cover with clingfilm and leave to marinate in the refrigerator for 6–8 hours.

Meanwhile, cream the butter in a bowl, then beat in the remaining cayenne pepper to taste. Cover the bowl with clingfilm and leave until you are ready to serve.

Preheat the grill. Place the turkey legs on a grill rack and cook under the grill, turning frequently, for 15–20 minutes, or until golden brown and cooked through. Test by inserting the point of a sharp knife in the thickest part. If the juices run clear, the turkey is cooked.

Transfer the turkey legs to a carving board and carve into slices. Arrange on a serving plate with the cayenne butter. Serve immediately.

Cheese Straws

makes 10–12

115 g/4 oz unsalted butter,
plus extra for greasing

115 g/4 oz plain flour, plus
extra for dusting

pinch of salt

pinch of paprika

1 tsp mustard powder

85 g/3 oz Cheddar or
Gruyère cheese, grated

1 egg, lightly beaten

1–2 tbsp cold water

poppy seeds, for coating

Preheat the oven to 200°C/400°F/Gas Mark 6. Lightly grease 2 baking sheets with butter.

Sift the flour, salt, paprika and mustard powder into a bowl. Add the remaining butter, cut it into the flour with a knife, then rub in with your fingertips until the mixture resembles breadcrumbs. Stir in the cheese and add half of the beaten egg, then mix in enough water to make a firm dough. The dough may be stored in the freezer. Thaw at room temperature before rolling out.

Spread out the poppy seeds on a plate. Turn the dough on to a lightly floured work surface and knead briefly, then roll out. Using a sharp knife, cut into strips measuring 10 x 0.5 cm/4 x ¼ inch. Brush with the remaining beaten egg and roll the straws in the poppy seeds to coat, then arrange them on the baking sheets. Gather up the dough trimmings and re-roll. Stamp out 10–12 rounds with a 6-cm/2½-inch fluted cutter, then stamp out the centres with a 5-cm/2-inch plain cutter. Brush with the egg and place on the baking sheets.

Bake in the preheated oven for 10 minutes until golden brown. Leave the cheese straws on the baking sheets to cool slightly, then transfer to wire racks to cool completely. Store in an airtight container. Thread the pastry straws through the pastry rings before serving.

Piquant Crab Bites

makes 50

100 g/3½ oz fresh white breadcrumbs

2 large eggs, separated

200 ml/7 fl oz crème fraîche

1 tsp English mustard powder

500 g/1 lb 2 oz fresh white crabmeat

1 tbsp chopped fresh dill

groundnut oil, for frying

salt and pepper

2 limes, quartered, to serve

Tip the breadcrumbs into a large bowl. In a separate bowl, whisk the egg yolks with the crème fraîche and mustard powder and add to the breadcrumbs with the crabmeat and dill, season to taste with salt and pepper and mix together well. Cover and chill in the refrigerator for 15 minutes.

In a clean bowl, whisk the egg whites until stiff. Lightly fold a tablespoonful of the egg whites into the crab mixture, then fold in the remaining egg whites.

Heat 2 tablespoons of oil in a non-stick frying pan over a medium–high heat. Drop in as many teaspoonfuls of the crab mixture as will fit in the frying pan without overcrowding, flatten slightly and cook for 2 minutes, or until brown and crisp. Flip over and cook for a further 1–2 minutes until the undersides are browned. Remove and drain on kitchen paper. Keep warm while you cook the remaining crab mixture, adding more oil to the frying pan if necessary.

Serve the crab bites warm with the lime quarters for squeezing over.

Scallops Wrapped in Pancetta

serves 12

12 fresh rosemary sprigs

6 raw scallops, corals removed

12 thin-cut pancetta rashers

dressing

2 tbsp olive oil

1 tbsp white wine vinegar

1 tsp honey

salt and pepper

First prepare the rosemary by stripping most of the leaves off the stalks, leaving a cluster of leaves at the top. Trim the stalks to about 6 cm/2½ inches long, cutting each sprig at an angle at the base.

Cut each scallop in half through the centre to give 2 discs of scallop, wrap each one in a pancetta rasher and, keeping the end tucked under, place on a plate. Cover and chill in the refrigerator for 15 minutes.

To make the dressing, whisk the oil, vinegar and honey together in a small bowl and season to taste with salt and pepper.

Preheat the grill to high or heat a ridged griddle pan over a high heat. Cook the scallops under the grill or on the griddle pan for 2 minutes on each side until the pancetta is crisp and brown. Spear each one on a prepared rosemary skewer and serve hot, with the dressing as a dip.

Corn & Parmesan Fritters

makes 25–30

5 fresh corn on the cob or 500 g/1 lb 2 oz frozen or canned sweetcorn kernels

2 eggs, beaten

4 tbsp plain flour

2 tbsp finely grated Parmesan cheese

1 tsp bicarbonate of soda

4 tbsp full-fat milk

vegetable oil, for frying

salt

If you are using fresh corn on the cobs, cook them in a large saucepan of boiling water for 7 minutes, then drain well. Stand them on their ends, cut away the kernels and leave to cool. If using frozen sweetcorn kernels, leave to thaw first, or drain canned sweetcorn kernels.

Put the sweetcorn kernels in a bowl with the eggs, flour, Parmesan cheese, bicarbonate of soda and a pinch of salt. Mix together, then add the milk and stir together well.

Heat the oil to a depth of 4 cm/1½ inches in a deep saucepan to a temperature of 180°C/350°F, or until a cube of bread browns in 30 seconds. Drop 4 teaspoonfuls of the mixture into the oil at a time and cook for 2 minutes. Turn over and cook for a further minute or so, or until crisp, brown and slightly puffed up. Remove and drain on kitchen paper. Keep warm while you cook the remaining batches of mixture – you may need to add a little more oil between batches and scoop out any stray sweetcorn kernels. Sprinkle with salt to serve.

Turkey Club Sandwiches

serves 6

sandwiches

12 pancetta or streaky
bacon rashers

18 slices white bread

12 slices cooked turkey
breast meat

3 plum tomatoes, sliced

6 Little Gem lettuce leaves

6 stuffed olives

salt and pepper

mayonnaise

2 large egg yolks

1 tsp English mustard
powder

1 tsp salt

300 ml/10 fl oz groundnut
oil

1 tsp white wine vinegar

pepper

First make the mayonnaise. Put the egg yolks in a bowl, add the mustard powder, pepper to taste and salt and beat together well. Pour the oil into a jug and make sure that your bowl is secure on the work surface by sitting it on a damp cloth. Using an electric or hand whisk, begin to whisk the egg yolks, adding just 1 drop of the oil. Make sure that this has been thoroughly absorbed before adding another drop and whisking well.

Continue adding the oil 1 drop at a time until the mixture thickens and stiffens – at this point, whisk in the vinegar and then continue to dribble in the remaining oil very slowly in a thin stream, whisking constantly, until you have used up all the oil and you have a thick mayonnaise. Cover and refrigerate while you prepare the other sandwich components.

Grill or fry the pancetta until crisp, drain on kitchen paper and keep warm. Toast the bread until golden, then cut off the crusts.

You will need 3 slices of toast for each sandwich. For each sandwich, spread the first piece of toast with a generous amount of mayonnaise, top with 2 slices of turkey, keeping the edges neat, and then top with a couple of slices of tomato. Season to taste with salt and pepper. Add another slice of toast and top with 2 pancetta rashers and 1 lettuce leaf. Season to taste again with salt and pepper, add a little more mayonnaise, then top with the final piece of toast. Push a cocktail stick or a decorative sparkler through a stuffed olive, and then push this through the sandwich to hold it together.

Main
Courses

Roast Turkey with Bread Sauce

serves 8

1 quantity Chestnut and
Sausage Stuffing

one 5-kg/11-lb turkey

40 g/1½ oz butter

bread sauce

1 onion, peeled

4 cloves

600 ml/1 pint milk

115 g/4 oz fresh white
breadcrumbs

55 g/2 oz butter

salt and pepper

Preheat the oven to 220°C/425°F/Gas Mark 7. If you are planning on stuffing the turkey, spoon the stuffing into the neck cavity and close the flap of skin with a skewer. If you prefer to cook the stuffing separately, cook according to the recipe's instructions.

Place the bird in a large roasting tin and rub it all over with the butter. Roast in the preheated oven for 1 hour, then lower the oven temperature to 180°C/350°F/Gas Mark 4 and roast for a further 2½ hours. You may need to pour off the fat from the roasting tin occasionally.

Meanwhile, make the bread sauce. Stud the onion with the cloves, then place in a saucepan with the milk, breadcrumbs and butter. Bring just to boiling point over a low heat, then remove from the heat and leave to stand in a warm place to infuse. Just before serving, remove the onion and cloves and reheat the sauce gently, beating well with a wooden spoon. Season to taste with salt and pepper.

Check that the turkey is cooked by inserting a skewer or the point of a sharp knife into the thigh – if the juices run clear, it is ready. Transfer the bird to a carving board, cover loosely with foil and leave to rest.

Carve the turkey and serve with the warm bread sauce and stuffing.

Yuletide Goose with Honey & Pears

serves 4–6

one 3.5–4.5-kg/7¾–10-lb oven-ready goose

1 tsp salt

4 pears

1 tbsp lemon juice

4 tbsp butter

2 tbsp honey

Preheat the oven to 220°C/425°F/Gas Mark 7. Rinse the goose and pat dry. Use a fork to prick the skin all over, then rub with the salt. Place the bird upside down on a rack in a roasting tin. Roast in the preheated oven for 30 minutes. Drain off the fat. Turn the bird over and roast for 15 minutes. Drain off the fat.

Reduce the heat to 180°C/350°F/Gas Mark 4 and roast for 15 minutes per 450 g/1 lb. Cover with foil 15 minutes before the end of the cooking time. Check that the bird is cooked by inserting a knife between the legs and body. If the juices run clear, it is cooked. Remove from the oven. Transfer the goose to a warmed serving platter, cover loosely with foil and leave to rest.

Peel and halve the pears, then brush with the lemon juice. Melt the butter and honey in a saucepan over a low heat, then add the pears. Cook, stirring, for 5–10 minutes until tender. Remove from the heat, arrange the pears around the goose and pour the sweet juices over the bird, then serve.

Glazed Gammon

serves 8

one 4-kg/8¾-lb gammon
joint

1 apple, cored and chopped

1 onion, chopped

300 ml/10 fl oz dry cider

6 black peppercorns

1 bouquet garni

1 bay leaf

about 50 cloves

4 tbsp Demerara sugar

Put the gammon in a large saucepan and add enough cold water to cover. Bring to the boil and skim off the scum that rises to the surface. Reduce the heat and simmer for 30 minutes. Drain the gammon and return to the saucepan. Add the apple, onion, cider, peppercorns, bouquet garni, bay leaf and a few of the cloves. Pour in enough fresh water to cover and return to the boil. Reduce the heat, cover and simmer for 3 hours 20 minutes.

Preheat the oven to 200°C/400°F/Gas Mark 6. Take the saucepan off the heat and set aside to cool slightly. Remove the gammon from the cooking liquid and, while it is still warm, loosen the rind with a sharp knife, then peel it off and discard. Score the fat into diamond shapes and stud with the remaining cloves. Place the gammon on a rack in a roasting tin and sprinkle with the sugar. Roast in the oven for 20 minutes, basting occasionally with the cooking liquid. Serve hot, or cold later.

Traditional Roast Chicken

serves 6

one 2.25-kg/5-lb free-range chicken

55 g/2 oz butter

2 tbsp chopped fresh lemon thyme

2 lemons, halved

125 ml/4 fl oz white wine

salt and pepper

6 fresh thyme sprigs, to garnish

Preheat the oven to 220°C/425°F/Gas Mark 7. Make sure the chicken is clean, wiping it inside and out with kitchen paper, and place in a roasting tin. In a bowl, soften the butter with a fork, mix in the thyme and season well with salt and pepper. Butter the chicken all over with the herb butter, inside and out, and place the lemon pieces inside the body cavity. Pour the wine over the chicken.

Roast in the centre of the preheated oven for 20 minutes. Reduce the temperature to 190°C/375°F/Gas Mark 5 and roast for a further 1¼ hours, basting frequently. Cover with foil if the skin begins to brown too much. If the tin dries out, add a little more wine or water.

Test that the chicken is cooked by piercing the thickest part of the leg with a sharp knife or skewer and making sure the juices run clear. Remove from the oven. Transfer the chicken to a warmed serving plate, cover loosely with foil and leave to rest for 10 minutes before carving. Remove the lemon halves and place around the sides of the plate. Place the roasting tin on the top of the stove and bubble the pan juices gently over a low heat until they have reduced and are thick and glossy. Season to taste with salt and pepper. Serve the chicken with the pan juices and scatter with the thyme sprigs.

Chicken Roulades

serves 6

6 skinless, boneless
chicken breasts, about
175 g/6 oz each

200 g/7 oz fresh chicken
mince

1 tbsp olive oil

2 shallots, roughly chopped

1 garlic clove, crushed

150 ml/5 fl oz double cream

3 fresh sage leaves,
chopped

1 tbsp chopped fresh
parsley

1 tbsp cognac or sherry

1 tbsp vegetable oil

18 pancetta rashers

1 dessertspoon plain flour

200 ml/7 fl oz white wine

200 ml/7 fl oz chicken stock

salt and pepper

rösti and gravy, to serve

Place a chicken breast between 2 pieces of clingfilm and, using a rolling pin, flatten the breast as evenly as possible. Trim off the rough edges to make a neat square. Repeat with the remaining breasts, cover and chill in the refrigerator.

Meanwhile, chop the chicken trimmings and mix with the mince in a bowl. Heat the olive oil in a small frying pan over a medium heat, add the shallots and garlic and cook, stirring frequently, for 5 minutes. Add to the mince with the cream, herbs and cognac and mix together thoroughly. Season to taste with salt and pepper, cover and chill in the refrigerator for 15 minutes.

Bring a large saucepan of water to the boil, then reduce to a simmer. Divide the mince mixture between the breasts, spread to within 1 cm/½ inch of the edge, and then roll each breast up to form a sausage shape. Wrap each roll tightly in kitchen foil, securing both ends. Poach in the simmering water for 20 minutes, remove with a slotted spoon and leave to cool completely.

Meanwhile, preheat the oven to 190°C/375°F/Gas Mark 5. Put the vegetable oil in a roasting tin and heat in the oven. Remove the kitchen foil and wrap each roulade tightly in 3 pancetta rashers. Carefully roll in the hot oil, then roast in the oven for 25–30 minutes, turning twice, until they are browned and crisp.

Remove the roulades from the tin and keep warm. Place the tin on the hob, add the flour and stir well with a wooden spoon to form a smooth paste. Gradually whisk in the wine and stock. Leave to bubble for 4–5 minutes, then season to taste. Slice the roulades and serve with rösti and gravy.

Quail with Grapes

serves 4

4 tbsp olive oil

8 quail, gutted

280 g/10 oz green seedless grapes

225 ml/8 fl oz grape juice

2 cloves

about 150 ml/5 fl oz water

2 tbsp Spanish brandy

salt and pepper

potato pancake

600 g/1 lb 5 oz unpeeled potatoes

35 g/1¼ oz unsalted butter or pork fat

1½ tbsp olive oil

Preheat the oven to 230°C/450°F/Gas Mark 8. For the pancake, parboil the potatoes for 10 minutes. Drain and leave to cool completely, then peel, coarsely grate and season with salt and pepper to taste. Reserve until required.

Take a heavy-based frying pan or flameproof casserole large enough to hold the quail in a single layer and heat the oil over a medium heat. Add the quail and fry on all sides until they are golden brown.

Add the grapes, grape juice, cloves, enough water to come halfway up the side of the quail, and salt and pepper to taste. Cover and simmer for 20 minutes. Transfer the quail and all the juices to a roasting tin or casserole, and sprinkle with brandy. Roast, uncovered, in the preheated oven for 10 minutes.

Meanwhile, to make the potato pancake, melt the butter with the oil in a 30-cm/12-inch non-stick frying pan over a high heat. When the fat is hot, add the grated potato and spread into an even layer. Reduce the heat and simmer for 10 minutes. Place a plate over the frying pan and, wearing oven gloves, invert them so the potato pancake drops on to the plate. Slide the potato back into the frying pan and continue cooking on the other side for 10 minutes, or until cooked through and crisp. Slide out of the frying pan and cut into 4 wedges. Keep the pancake warm until the quail are ready.

Place a pancake wedge and 2 quail on each individual serving plate. Taste the grape sauce and adjust the seasoning if necessary. Spoon the sauce over the quail and serve immediately.

Duck with Madeira & Blueberry Sauce

serves 4

4 duck breasts (skin left on)

4 garlic cloves, chopped

grated rind and juice of
1 orange

1 tbsp chopped fresh
parsley

salt and pepper

new potatoes & selection of
green vegetables,
to serve

Madeira & blueberry sauce

150 g/5½ oz blueberries

250 ml/9 fl oz Madeira

1 tbsp redcurrant jelly

Use a sharp knife to make several shallow diagonal cuts in each duck breast. Put the duck in a glass bowl with the garlic, orange rind and juice, and the parsley. Season to taste with salt and pepper and stir well. Turn the duck in the mixture until thoroughly coated. Cover the bowl with clingfilm and leave in the refrigerator to marinate for at least 1 hour.

Heat a dry, non-stick frying pan over a medium heat. Add the duck breasts and cook for 4 minutes, then turn them over and cook for a further 4 minutes, or according to taste. Remove from the heat, cover the frying pan and leave to stand for 5 minutes.

Halfway through the cooking time, put the blueberries, Madeira and redcurrant jelly into a separate saucepan. Bring to the boil. Reduce the heat and simmer for 10 minutes, then remove from the heat.

Slice the duck breasts and transfer to warmed serving plates. Serve with the sauce poured over and accompanied by new potatoes and a selection of green vegetables.

Roast Duck with Apple Wedges

serves 4

4 duckling portions, about 350 g/12 oz each

4 tbsp dark soy sauce

2 tbsp light muscovado sugar

2 red-skinned apples

2 green-skinned apples

juice of 1 lemon

2 tbsp clear honey

a few bay leaves

salt and pepper

freshly cooked vegetables, to serve

for the apricot sauce

400 g/14 oz canned apricots in fruit juice

4 tbsp sweet sherry

Preheat the oven to 190°C/375°F/Gas Mark 5. Wash the duck and trim away any excess fat. Place on a wire rack over a roasting tin and prick all over with a fork or a clean, sharp needle.

Brush the duck with the soy sauce. Sprinkle over the sugar and season with pepper. Cook in the preheated oven, basting occasionally, for 50–60 minutes, or until the meat is cooked through and the juices run clear when a skewer is inserted into the thickest part of the meat.

Meanwhile, core the apples and cut each into 6 wedges, then place in a small bowl and mix with the lemon juice and honey. Transfer to a small roasting tin, add a few bay leaves and season to taste with salt and pepper. Cook alongside the duck, basting occasionally, for 20–25 minutes until tender. Discard the bay leaves.

To make the sauce, place the apricots in a blender or food processor with the can juices and the sherry. Process until smooth. Alternatively, mash the apricots with a fork until smooth and mix with the juice and sherry.

Just before serving, heat the apricot sauce in a small saucepan. Remove the skin from the duck and pat the flesh with kitchen paper to absorb any fat. Serve the duck with the apple wedges, apricot sauce and freshly cooked vegetables.

Festive Beef Wellington

serves 4

750 g/1 lb 10 oz thick beef fillet

2 tbsp butter

2 tbsp vegetable oil

1 garlic clove, chopped

1 onion, chopped

175 g/6 oz chestnut mushrooms, thinly sliced

1 tbsp chopped fresh sage

350 g/12 oz puff pastry, thawed if frozen

1 egg, beaten

salt and pepper

Preheat the oven to 220°C/425°F/Gas Mark 7. Put the beef in a roasting tin, spread with the butter and season to taste with salt and pepper. Roast in the preheated oven for 30 minutes, then remove from the oven.

Meanwhile, heat the oil in a saucepan over a medium heat. Add the garlic and onion and cook, stirring, for 3 minutes. Stir in salt and pepper to taste, the mushrooms and the sage and cook, stirring frequently, for 5 minutes. Remove from the heat.

Roll out the pastry into a rectangle large enough to enclose the beef, then place the beef in the centre and spread the mushroom mixture over it. Bring the long sides of the pastry together over the beef and seal with beaten egg. Tuck the short ends over (trim away excess pastry) and seal. Place on a baking sheet, seam-side down. Make 2 slits in the top. Decorate with dough shapes and brush with egg. Bake for 40 minutes. Remove from the oven, cut into thick slices and serve.

Roast Pheasant with Wine & Herbs

serves 4

100 g/3½ oz butter, slightly softened

1 tbsp chopped fresh thyme

1 tbsp chopped fresh parsley

2 oven-ready young pheasants

4 tbsp vegetable oil

125 ml/4 fl oz red wine

salt and pepper

game chips, to serve

Preheat the oven to 190°C/375°F/Gas Mark 5. Put the butter in a small bowl and mix in the chopped herbs. Lift the skin away from the breasts of the pheasants, taking care not to tear it, and push the herb butter under the skins. Season to taste with salt and pepper. Pour the oil into a roasting tin, add the pheasants and roast in the preheated oven for 45 minutes, basting occasionally. Remove from the oven, pour over the wine, then return to the oven and cook for a further 15 minutes, or until cooked through. Check that each bird is cooked by inserting a knife between the legs and body. If the juices run clear, they are cooked.

Remove the pheasants from the oven, cover loosely with foil and leave to rest for 15 minutes. Serve on a warmed serving platter surrounded by game chips.

Steak with Pancakes & Mustard Sauce

serves 6

vegetable oil, for frying

6 fillet steaks, about
150 g/5½ oz each

1 tbsp olive oil

1 tsp unsalted butter

200 ml/7 fl oz crème fraîche

2 tsp wholegrain mustard

salt and pepper

2 tbsp snipped fresh chives,
to garnish

pancakes

400 g/14 oz potatoes

55 g/2 oz self-raising flour

½ tsp baking powder

200 ml/7 fl oz milk

2 eggs, beaten

To make the pancakes, cook the potatoes in their skins in a large saucepan of boiling water until tender. Drain and leave until cool enough to handle. Peel, then pass through a potato ricer, or mash and press through a sieve, into a bowl.

Sift the flour and baking powder over the potatoes, then add a little of the milk and mix well. Add the remaining milk and the eggs and beat well to make a smooth batter.

Heat a little vegetable oil in a 20-cm/8-inch non-stick frying pan over a medium heat. Add a ladleful of the batter to cover the base of the pan and cook until little bubbles appear on the surface. Turn over and cook for a further minute, or until nicely browned, then turn out and keep warm. Repeat until you have cooked 6 pancakes.

Season the steaks to taste with salt and pepper. Heat the olive oil and butter in a non-stick frying pan over a high heat until sizzling. Add the fillet steaks and cook to your liking, then remove from the pan and keep warm. Add the crème fraîche and mustard to the pan, stir and heat through. Season well with salt and pepper. Serve each steak with a folded pancake and some sauce, scattered with a few snipped chives.

Lamb with Roquefort & Walnut Butter

serves 4

55 g/2 oz unsalted butter

140 g/5 oz Roquefort
cheese, crumbled

2 tbsp finely chopped
walnuts

8 lamb noisettes

salt and pepper

snipped chives, to garnish
(optional)

freshly cooked vegetables,
to serve

Cream half the butter in a bowl with a wooden spoon. Beat in the cheese and walnuts until thoroughly combined and season to taste with salt and pepper. Turn out the flavoured butter onto a sheet of greaseproof paper and shape into a cylinder. Wrap and leave to chill in the refrigerator until firm.

Heat a ridged griddle pan, add the remaining butter and as soon as it has melted, add the lamb noisettes. Then cook for 4–5 minutes on each side.

Transfer the lamb to warmed serving plates and top each noisette with a slice of Roquefort and walnut butter. Serve immediately with snipped chives, to garnish, if using, and freshly cooked vegetables.

Herbed Salmon with Hollandaise Sauce

serves 4

4 salmon fillets, about
175 g/6 oz each, skin
removed

2 tbsp olive oil

1 tbsp chopped fresh dill

1 tbsp snipped fresh chives,
plus extra to garnish

salt and pepper

freshly cooked sprouting
broccoli and sesame
seeds, to serve

hollandaise sauce

3 egg yolks

1 tbsp water

225 g/8 oz butter, cut into
small cubes

juice of 1 lemon

salt and pepper

Preheat the grill to medium. Rinse the fish fillets under cold running water and pat dry with kitchen paper. Season to taste with salt and pepper. Combine the oil with the dill and chives in a bowl, then brush the mixture over the fish. Transfer to the grill and cook for 6–8 minutes, turning once and brushing with more oil and herb mixture, until cooked to your taste.

Meanwhile, make the sauce. Put the egg yolks in a heatproof bowl over a saucepan of gently simmering water (or use a double boiler). Add the water and season to taste with salt and pepper. Reduce the heat until the water in the saucepan is barely simmering and whisk constantly until the mixture begins to thicken. Whisk in the butter, one piece at a time, until the mixture is thick and shiny. Whisk in the lemon juice, then remove from the heat.

Remove the salmon from the grill and transfer to warmed individual serving plates. Pour the sauce over the fish and garnish with snipped fresh chives. Serve immediately on a bed of sprouting broccoli, garnished with sesame seeds.

Poached Salmon

serves 8–12

4 litres/7 pints water

6 tbsp white wine vinegar

1 large onion, sliced

2 carrots, sliced

1½ tbsp salt

1 tsp black peppercorns

one 2.7-kg/6-lb salmon, cleaned, with gills and eyes removed

fresh dill, to garnish

salad, to serve

To make a court-bouillon (stock) in which to poach the fish, put the water, vinegar, onion, carrots, salt and peppercorns in a large fish kettle or covered roasting tin and bring to the boil. Reduce the heat and simmer for 20 minutes. Remove the trivet (if using a fish kettle) and lay the salmon on it. Lower it into the court-bouillon, cover, return to simmering point and cook for 5 minutes. Turn off the heat and leave the fish, covered, to cool in the liquid.

When the fish is cold, lift it out of the kettle on the trivet and drain well. Using 2 fish slices, carefully transfer to a board. Using a sharp knife, remove the head, then slit the skin along the backbone and peel off. Carefully turn the fish over and peel off the skin on the other side.

Garnish with dill and serve with salad.

Smoked Salmon Risotto

serves 4

50 g/1¾ oz unsalted butter

1 onion, finely chopped

½ small fennel bulb, very finely chopped

500 g/1 lb 2 oz arborio or carnaroli rice

300 ml/10 fl oz white wine or vermouth

1.2 litres/2 pints hot fish stock

150 g/5½ oz hot smoked salmon flakes

150 g/5½ oz smoked salmon slices

2 tbsp fresh chervil leaves or chopped flat-leaf parsley

salt and pepper

Melt half the butter in a large saucepan over a medium heat, add the onion and fennel and cook, stirring frequently, for 5–8 minutes until transparent and soft. Add the rice and stir well to coat the grains in the butter. Cook, stirring, for 3 minutes, then add the wine, stir and leave to simmer until most of the liquid has been absorbed.

With the stock simmering in a separate saucepan, add 1 ladleful to the rice and stir well. Cook, stirring constantly, until nearly all the liquid has been absorbed before adding another ladleful of stock. Continue to add the remaining stock in the same way until the rice is cooked al dente and most or all of the stock has been added.

Remove from the heat and stir in the two types of salmon and the remaining butter, season to taste with salt and pepper and serve scattered with the chervil.

Mixed Nut Roast

serves 4

2 tbsp butter, plus extra for greasing

2 garlic cloves, chopped

1 large onion, chopped

50 g/1¾ oz pine kernels, toasted

75 g/2¾ oz hazelnuts, toasted

50 g/1¾ oz walnuts, ground

50 g/1¾ oz cashew nuts, ground

100 g/3½ oz fresh wholemeal breadcrumbs

1 egg, lightly beaten

2 tbsp chopped fresh thyme

250 ml/9 fl oz vegetable stock

salt and pepper

fresh thyme sprigs, to garnish

cranberry sauce, to serve

Preheat the oven to 180°C/350°F/Gas Mark 4. Grease a loaf tin with butter and line it with greaseproof paper. Melt the remaining butter in a saucepan over a medium heat. Add the garlic and onion and cook, stirring, for 5 minutes, until softened. Remove from the heat. Grind the pine kernels and hazelnuts. Stir all the nuts into the saucepan, add the breadcrumbs, egg, thyme and stock and season to taste with salt and pepper.

Spoon the mixture into the loaf tin and level the surface. Cook in the preheated oven for 30 minutes, or until cooked through and golden. The loaf is cooked when a skewer inserted into the centre comes out clean.

Remove the nut roast from the oven and turn out onto a warmed serving dish. Garnish with thyme sprigs and serve with cranberry sauce.

Cheese & Vegetable Tart

serves 4

350 g/12 oz ready-made shortcrust pastry, thawed if frozen

280 g/10 oz mixed frozen vegetables

150 ml/5 fl oz double cream

115 g/4 oz Cheddar cheese, grated

salt and pepper

Thinly roll out the dough on a lightly floured work surface and use to line a 23-cm/9-inch quiche tin. Prick the base and chill in the refrigerator for 30 minutes. Preheat the oven to 200°C/400°F/Gas Mark 6.

Line the pastry case with foil and half-fill with baking beans. Place the tin on a baking sheet and bake for 15–20 minutes, or until just firm. Remove the beans and foil, return the pastry case to the oven and bake for a further 5–7 minutes until golden. Remove the pastry case from the oven and leave to cool in the tin.

Meanwhile, cook the frozen vegetables in a saucepan of salted boiling water. Drain and leave to cool.

When ready to cook, preheat the oven again to 200°C/ 400°F/Gas Mark 6. Mix the cooked vegetables and cream together and season with salt and pepper. Spoon the mixture evenly into the pastry case and sprinkle with the cheese. Bake for 15 minutes, or until the cheese has melted and is turning golden. Serve hot or cold.

Accompaniments

Perfect Roast Potatoes

serves 8

70 g/2½ oz goose or duck fat or 5 tbsp olive oil

1 kg/2 lb 4 oz even-sized potatoes, peeled

coarse sea salt

8 fresh rosemary sprigs, to garnish

Preheat the oven to 230°C/450°F/Gas Mark 8. Put the fat in a large roasting tin, sprinkle generously with sea salt and place in the oven.

Meanwhile, cook the potatoes in a large saucepan of boiling water for 8–10 minutes until parboiled. Drain well and, if the potatoes are large, cut them in half. Return the potatoes to the empty saucepan and shake vigorously to roughen their outsides.

Arrange the potatoes in a single layer in the hot fat and roast for 45 minutes. If they look as if they are beginning to char around the edges, reduce the oven temperature to 200°C/400°F/Gas Mark 6. Turn the potatoes over and roast for a further 30 minutes until crisp. Serve garnished with rosemary sprigs.

Two-potato Purée

serves 6

2 large orange sweet
potatoes

½ tsp vegetable oil

4 potatoes

25 g/1 oz butter

125 ml/4 fl oz double cream

whole nutmeg, for grating

salt and pepper

Preheat the oven to 190°C/375°F/Gas Mark 5. Rub the sweet potatoes with the oil, then bake in the preheated oven for 20–25 minutes until tender.

Meanwhile, peel the potatoes, then cook in a large saucepan of boiling water until tender. Drain well and put in a colander. Cover with a clean tea towel to absorb the steam and leave to stand until cooled. Mash the potatoes or pass through a potato ricer.

Scoop out the flesh from the sweet potatoes and mix well with the potato in a warmed bowl. Discard the sweet potato skins. Melt the butter with the cream in a small saucepan, then pour half over the potato mixture and beat well with a wooden spoon. Add the remaining cream mixture a little at a time until you achieve the consistency you like. Season to taste with salt and pepper, and add a grating of nutmeg. Beat again, then serve.

Garlic Mash

serves 4

900 g/2 lb floury potatoes, cut into chunks

8 garlic cloves, crushed

150 ml/5 fl oz milk

85 g/3 oz butter

pinch of freshly grated nutmeg

salt and pepper

Place the potatoes in a large saucepan with enough water to cover and a pinch of salt. Bring to the boil and cook for 10 minutes. Add the garlic and cook for a further 10–15 minutes, or until the potatoes are tender.

Drain the potatoes and garlic, reserving 3 tablespoons of the cooking liquid. Return the reserved cooking liquid to the saucepan, then add the milk and bring to simmering point. Add the butter, return the potatoes and garlic to the saucepan and turn off the heat. Mash thoroughly with a potato masher.

Season the potato mixture to taste with nutmeg, salt and pepper and beat thoroughly with a wooden spoon until light and fluffy. Serve immediately.

Buttered Brussels Sprouts with Chestnuts

serves 4

350 g/12 oz Brussels sprouts, trimmed

3 tbsp butter

100 g/3½ oz canned whole chestnuts

pinch of grated nutmeg

salt and pepper

50 g/1¾ oz flaked almonds, to garnish

Bring a large saucepan of salted water to the boil. Add the Brussels sprouts and cook for 5 minutes. Drain thoroughly.

Melt the butter in a large saucepan over a medium heat. Add the Brussels sprouts and cook, stirring, for 3 minutes, then add the chestnuts and nutmeg. Season to taste with salt and pepper and stir well. Cook for a further 2 minutes, stirring, then remove from the heat. Transfer to a warmed serving dish, scatter over the almonds and serve.

Sugar-glazed Parsnips

serves 8

24 small parsnips, peeled

about 1 tsp salt

115 g/4 oz butter

115 g/4 oz soft brown sugar

Place the parsnips in a saucepan, add just enough water to cover, then add the salt. Bring to the boil, reduce the heat, cover and simmer for 20–25 minutes, until tender. Drain well.

Melt the butter in a heavy frying pan or wok. Add the parsnips and toss well. Sprinkle with the sugar, then cook, stirring frequently to prevent the sugar from sticking to the pan or burning. Cook the parsnips for 10–15 minutes, until golden and glazed. Transfer to a warm serving dish and serve immediately.

Spiced Winter Vegetables

serves 4

4 parsnips, scrubbed and trimmed but left unpeeled

4 carrots, scrubbed and trimmed but left unpeeled

2 onions, quartered

1 red onion, quartered

3 leeks, trimmed and cut into 6-cm/2½-inch slices

6 garlic cloves, left unpeeled and whole

6 tbsp extra virgin olive oil

½ tsp mild chilli powder

pinch of paprika

salt and pepper

Preheat the oven to 220°C/425°F/Gas Mark 7. Bring a large saucepan of water to the boil.

Cut the parsnips and carrots into wedges of similar size. Add them to the saucepan and cook for 5 minutes. Drain thoroughly and place in an ovenproof dish with the onions, leeks and garlic. Pour over the oil, sprinkle in the spices and salt and pepper to taste, then mix until all the vegetables are well coated.

Roast in the preheated oven for at least 1 hour. Turn the vegetables from time to time until they are tender and starting to colour. Remove from the oven, transfer to a warmed serving dish and serve immediately.

Garlic Mushrooms with White Wine & Chestnuts

serves 4

55 g/2 oz butter

4 garlic cloves, chopped

200 g/7 oz button
mushrooms, sliced

200 g/7 oz chestnut
mushrooms, sliced

4 tbsp dry white wine

100 ml/3½ fl oz double
cream

300 g/10½ oz canned whole
chestnuts, drained

100 g/3½ oz chanterelle
mushrooms, sliced

salt and pepper

chopped fresh parsley,
to garnish

Melt the butter in a large saucepan over a medium heat. Add the garlic and cook, stirring, for 3 minutes, until softened. Add the button and chestnut mushrooms and cook for 3 minutes.

Stir in the wine and cream and season to taste with salt and pepper. Cook for 2 minutes, stirring, then add the chestnuts and the chanterelle mushrooms. Cook for a further 2 minutes, stirring, then remove from the heat and transfer to a warmed serving dish. Garnish with chopped fresh parsley and serve.

Honey-glazed Red Cabbage with Sultanas

serves 4

2 tbsp butter

1 garlic clove, chopped

650 g/1 lb 7 oz red cabbage, shredded

150 g/5½ oz sultanas

1 tbsp clear honey

100 ml/3½ fl oz red wine

100 ml/3½ fl oz water

Melt the butter in a large saucepan over a medium heat. Add the garlic and cook, stirring, for 1 minute, until slightly softened.

Add the cabbage and sultanas, then stir in the honey. Cook for 1 minute more. Pour in the wine and water and bring to the boil. Reduce the heat, cover and simmer gently, stirring occasionally, for 45 minutes, or until the cabbage is cooked. Serve hot.

Wild Mushroom Filo Parcels

serves 6

30 g/1 oz dried porcini mushrooms

70 g/2½ oz butter

1 shallot, finely chopped

1 garlic clove, crushed

100 g/3½ oz chestnut mushrooms, sliced

100 g/3½ oz white cap mushrooms, sliced

200 g/7 oz wild mushrooms, roughly chopped

150 g/5½ oz basmati rice, cooked and cooled

2 tbsp dry sherry

1 tbsp soy sauce or mushroom sauce

1 tbsp chopped fresh flat-leaf parsley

18 sheets filo pastry, thawed if frozen

vegetable oil, for oiling

350 ml/12 fl oz crème fraîche

50 ml/2 fl oz Madeira

salt and pepper

Put the dried mushrooms in a heatproof bowl and just cover with boiling water. Leave to soak for 20 minutes.

Meanwhile, melt half the butter in a large frying pan over a low heat, add the shallot and garlic and cook, stirring occasionally, for 5–8 minutes until the shallot is transparent and soft. Add all the fresh mushrooms and cook, stirring, for 2–3 minutes.

Preheat the oven to 200°C/400°F/Gas Mark 6. Drain the dried mushrooms, reserving the soaking liquid, roughly chop and add to the frying pan with the rice, sherry, soy sauce and parsley. Season well with salt and pepper, mix together well and simmer until most of the liquid has evaporated.

Melt the remaining butter in a small saucepan. Lay 1 sheet of filo pastry on a work surface and brush with melted butter. Put another sheet on top and brush with butter, then top with a third sheet. Spoon some of the mushroom mixture into the centre, then fold in the edges to form a parcel. Use a little more of the melted butter to make sure that the edges are secure. Repeat to make 6 parcels.

Place the parcels on a lightly oiled baking sheet and brush with the remaining melted butter. Bake in the preheated oven for 25–30 minutes until golden.

Meanwhile, to make the sauce, heat the reserved soaking liquid in a saucepan, add the crème fraîche and Madeira and stir over a low heat until heated through. Season to taste with salt and pepper and serve with the parcels.

Chestnut & Sausage Stuffing

serves 6–8

225 g/8 oz pork sausage meat

225 g/8 oz unsweetened chestnut purée

85 g/3 oz walnuts, chopped

115 g/4 oz ready-to-eat dried apricots, chopped

2 tbsp chopped fresh parsley

2 tbsp snipped fresh chives

2 tsp chopped fresh sage

4–5 tbsp double cream

salt and pepper

Combine the sausage meat and chestnut purée in a bowl, then stir in the walnuts, apricots, parsley, chives and sage. Stir in enough cream to make a firm, but not dry, mixture. Season to taste with salt and pepper.

If you are planning to stuff a turkey or goose, fill the neck cavity only to ensure the bird cooks all the way through. It is safer and more reliable to cook the stuffing separately, either rolled into small balls and placed on a baking sheet or spooned into an ovenproof dish.

Cook the separate stuffing in a preheated oven for 30–40 minutes at 190°C/375°F/Gas Mark 5. It should be allowed a longer time to cook if you are roasting a bird at a lower temperature in the same oven.

Pork, Cranberry & Herb Stuffing

serves 6

1 tbsp vegetable oil, plus extra for oiling

1 onion, finely chopped

2 celery sticks, chopped

450 g/1 lb pork sausage meat

50 g/1¾ oz fresh white or wholemeal breadcrumbs

50 g/1¾ oz dried cranberries

70 g/2½ oz fresh cranberries

1 tbsp chopped fresh parsley

1 tbsp chopped fresh sage

1 tbsp chopped fresh thyme leaves

1 large egg, beaten

salt and pepper

Heat the oil in a heavy-based frying pan over a medium heat, add the onion and celery and cook, stirring frequently, for 10 minutes until the onion is transparent and soft.

Meanwhile, preheat the oven to 190°C/375°F/Gas Mark 5. Break up the sausage meat in a large bowl. Add the breadcrumbs, dried and fresh cranberries and the herbs and mix together well. Add the cooked onion and celery, then the egg. Season well with salt and pepper and mix together thoroughly.

Form the stuffing into balls, place on an oiled baking sheet and bake in the preheated oven for 25 minutes. Alternatively, spoon into 2 foil tins, level the surface and bake for 45 minutes.

Bacon-wrapped Sausages

serves 4

8 pork sausages

2 tbsp mild mustard

24 ready-to-eat prunes

8 rashers smoked bacon

Preheat the grill. Using a sharp knife, cut a slit along the length of each sausage about three-quarters of the way through. Spread the mustard inside the slits and press 3 prunes into each sausage.

Stretch the bacon with the back of a knife until each rasher is quite thin. Wrap a rasher of bacon around each sausage.

Place the sausages on a grill rack and cook under the grill, turning occasionally, for 15–20 minutes until cooked through and browned all over. Serve immediately.

Festive Jewelled Rice

serves 6

250 g/9 oz basmati rice

70 g/2½ oz red or wild rice

70 g/2½ oz ready-to-eat
dried apricots

25 g/1 oz almonds,
blanched

25 g/1 oz hazelnuts, toasted

1 fresh red chilli, deseeded
and finely chopped

seeds of 1 pomegranate

1 tbsp finely chopped fresh
parsley

1 tbsp finely chopped fresh
mint

1 tbsp finely snipped fresh
chives

2 tbsp white wine vinegar

6 tbsp extra virgin olive oil

1 shallot, finely chopped

salt and pepper

Cook the two types of rice separately according to the packet instructions. Drain and leave to cool, then tip into a large bowl.

Chop the apricots and nuts and add to the rice with the chilli, pomegranate seeds and the herbs. Mix together well.

Just before you are ready to serve, whisk the vinegar, oil and shallot together in a jug and season well with salt and pepper. Pour the dressing over the rice and mix well. Pile into a serving dish.

Cranberry Sauce

serves 8

thinly pared rind and juice
of 1 lemon

thinly pared rind and juice
of 1 orange

350 g/12 oz cranberries,
thawed if frozen

140 g/5 oz caster sugar

2 tbsp arrowroot, mixed
with 3 tbsp cold water

Cut the strips of lemon and orange rind into thin shreds and place in a heavy-based saucepan. If using fresh cranberries, rinse well and remove any stalks. Add the berries, citrus juice and sugar to the saucepan and cook over a medium heat, stirring occasionally, for 5 minutes, or until the berries begin to burst.

Strain the juice into a clean saucepan and reserve the cranberries. Stir the arrowroot mixture into the juice, then bring to the boil, stirring constantly, until the sauce is smooth and thickened. Remove from the heat and stir in the reserved cranberries.

Transfer the cranberry sauce to a bowl and leave to cool, then cover with clingfilm and chill in the refrigerator.

Apple & Date Chutney

*makes one 300-g/
10½-oz jar*

175 ml/6 fl oz cider vinegar

1 shallot, finely chopped

1 cooking apple, peeled,
cored and chopped

¼ tsp ground allspice

300 g/10½ oz Medjool
dates, stoned and
chopped

5 tbsp honey

Put the vinegar, shallot, apple and allspice in a saucepan and bring to the boil. Reduce the heat and simmer for 5–8 minutes. Add the dates and honey and cook for 8–10 minutes until the dates are soft and the liquid is syrupy.

Remove from the heat and leave to cool. Serve straight away or pack into sterilized jars and store in the refrigerator.

Pickled Apricots with Star Anise

*makes two 500-g/
1-lb-2-oz jars*

500 ml/18 fl oz cider
vinegar

500 g/1 lb 2 oz unrefined
caster sugar

500 g/1 lb 2 oz ready-to-eat
dried apricots

2 dried chillies

4 star anise

Heat the vinegar and sugar in a saucepan over a medium heat, stirring until all the sugar has dissolved. Add the apricots, chillies and star anise to the saucepan and bring to the boil. Reduce the heat and simmer for 15 minutes until the syrup has thickened.

Ladle the apricots into sterilized jars and cover with the syrup. Leave to cool, then seal the jars and store in a dark, cool place for up to 2 weeks.

Desserts &
After-Dinner
Treats

Rich Christmas Pudding

serves 10–12

200 g/7 oz currants

200 g/7 oz raisins

200 g/7 oz sultanas

150 ml/5 fl oz sweet sherry

175 g/6 oz butter, plus extra for greasing

175 g/6 oz brown sugar

4 eggs, beaten

150 g/5½ oz self-raising flour

100 g/3½ oz fresh white or wholemeal breadcrumbs

50 g/1¾ oz blanched almonds, chopped

juice of 1 orange

grated rind of ½ orange

grated rind of ½ lemon

½ tsp mixed spice

holly, to decorate

icing sugar, for dusting

Put the currants, raisins and sultanas in a glass bowl and pour the sherry over. Cover and leave to soak for at least 2 hours.

Beat together the butter and brown sugar in a bowl. Beat in the eggs, then fold in the flour. Stir in the soaked fruit and the sherry with the breadcrumbs, almonds, orange juice and rind, lemon rind and mixed spice. Grease a 1.2-litre/2-pint pudding basin and spoon the mixture into it, packing it down well and leaving a gap of 2.5 cm/1 inch at the top. Cut a round of greaseproof paper 3 cm/1½ inches larger than the top of the basin, grease with butter and place over the pudding. Secure with string, then top with 2 layers of foil. Place the pudding in a saucepan filled with boiling water that reaches two-thirds of the way up the basin. Reduce the heat and simmer for 6 hours, topping up the water in the saucepan when necessary.

Remove from the heat and leave to cool. Renew the greaseproof paper and foil and store in the refrigerator for 2–8 weeks. To reheat, steam as before for 2 hours. Decorate with holly and a dusting of icing sugar.

Traditional Brandy Butter

serves 6–8

115 g/4 oz unsalted butter, at room temperature

55 g/2 oz caster sugar

55 g/2 oz icing sugar, sifted

3 tbsp brandy

Cream the butter in a bowl until it is very smooth and soft. Gradually beat in both types of sugar. Add the brandy, a little at a time, beating well after each addition and taking care not to let the mixture curdle.

Spread out the butter on a sheet of foil, cover and chill in the refrigerator until firm. Keep chilled until ready to serve.

Festive Sherry Trifle

serves 4–6

100 g/3½ oz trifle sponges

raspberry jam, for
spreading

150 ml/5 fl oz sherry

150 g/5½ oz frozen
raspberries, thawed

350 g/12 oz fresh
strawberries, sliced

custard

6 egg yolks

50 g/1¾ oz caster sugar

500 ml/18 fl oz milk

1 tsp vanilla extract

topping

300 ml/10 fl oz double
cream

1–2 tbsp caster sugar

1 chocolate bar, crumbled

Spread the trifle sponges with jam, cut them into bite-sized cubes and arrange in the bottom of a large glass serving bowl. Pour over the sherry and leave to stand for 30 minutes.

Combine the raspberries and strawberries and spoon them over the sponges in the bowl.

To make the custard, put the egg yolks and sugar into a bowl and whisk together. Pour the milk into a saucepan and warm gently over a low heat. Remove from the heat and gradually stir into the egg mixture, then return the mixture to the saucepan and stir constantly over a low heat until thickened. Do not boil. Remove from the heat, pour into a bowl and stir in the vanilla. Leave to cool for 1 hour. Spread the custard over the trifle, cover with clingfilm and chill in the refrigerator for 2 hours.

To make the topping, whip the cream in a bowl and stir in the sugar to taste. Spread the cream over the trifle, and then scatter over the chocolate pieces. Chill in the refrigerator for 30 minutes before serving.

Christmas Cake

*makes one 20-cm/
8-inch cake*

150 g/5½ oz raisins

125 g/4½ oz stoned dried
dates, chopped

125 g/4½ oz sultanas

100 g/3½ oz glacé cherries,
rinsed

150 ml/5 fl oz brandy

225 g/8 oz butter, plus extra
for greasing

200 g/7 oz caster sugar

4 eggs

grated rind of 1 orange

grated rind of 1 lemon

1 tbsp black treacle

225 g/8 oz plain flour

½ tsp salt

½ tsp baking powder

1 tsp mixed spice

25 g/1 oz toasted almonds,
chopped

25 g/1 oz toasted hazelnuts,
chopped

750 g/1 lb 10 oz marzipan

3 tbsp apricot jam, warmed

3 egg whites

650 g/1 lb 7 oz icing sugar

silver dragées, to decorate

Make this cake at least 3 weeks in advance. Put all the fruit in a bowl and pour over the brandy. Cover and leave to soak overnight.

Preheat the oven to 110°C/225°F/Gas Mark ¼. Grease a 20-cm/8-inch cake tin with butter and line it with greaseproof paper. Cream the remaining butter and the sugar in a bowl until fluffy. Gradually beat in the eggs. Stir in the citrus rind and treacle. Sift the flour, salt, baking powder and mixed spice into a separate bowl, then fold into the egg mixture. Fold in the soaked fruit and brandy and the nuts, then spoon the mixture into the cake tin.

Bake in the preheated oven for at least 3 hours. If it browns too quickly, cover with foil. The cake is cooked when a skewer inserted into the centre comes out clean. Remove from the oven and leave to cool on a wire rack. Store in an airtight container until required.

Roll out the marzipan and cut to shape to cover the top and sides of the cake. Brush the cake with the jam and press the marzipan on to the surface. Make the icing by placing the egg whites in a bowl and adding the icing sugar a little at a time, beating well until the icing is very thick and will stand up in peaks. Spread over the covered cake, using a fork to give texture. Decorate as you wish with silver dragées.

Christmas Frosted Ginger Cake

serves 6–8

175 g/6 oz unsalted butter, softened, plus extra for greasing

175 g/6 oz unrefined caster sugar

3 large eggs, beaten

1 tbsp black treacle

2 tbsp ginger syrup

225 g/8 oz self-raising flour

1 tsp ground ginger

1 tsp ground mixed spice

1 tbsp ground almonds

2 tbsp full-fat milk

70 g/2½ oz stem ginger, chopped

edible gold leaf or silver leaf, to decorate

icing

225 g/8 oz white icing sugar

1 tsp ginger syrup

Preheat the oven to 160°C/325°F/Gas Mark 3. Grease a 15 x 25-cm/6 x 10-inch square cake tin and line with greaseproof paper.

Cream the butter and caster sugar in a large bowl until pale and fluffy. Put the eggs and treacle into a jug with the ginger syrup and whisk together. Sift the flour and spices on to a plate. Alternately add a little of the egg mixture and then a spoonful of the flour mixture to the butter and sugar mixture until you have used up both. Add the almonds and milk and mix together until you have a smooth mixture. Fold in the stem ginger pieces.

Spoon the cake mixture into the prepared tin, smooth the surface with a palette knife and bake in the preheated oven for 45–50 minutes until well risen and firm to the touch. Leave to cool in the tin for 10 minutes, then turn out on to a wire rack to cool completely.

To make the icing, put the icing sugar in a large bowl. Beat in the ginger syrup and just enough cold water to make a thick icing – be careful not to add too much water too quickly. Remove the cake from the tin and spread the icing over the top, letting it run down the sides. Decorate with edible gold or silver leaf.

Dark Chocolate Yule Log

serves 8

butter, for greasing

115 g/4 oz self-raising flour,
plus extra for dusting

150 g/5½ oz caster sugar,
plus extra for sprinkling

4 eggs, separated

1 tsp almond extract

280 g/10 oz plain chocolate,
broken into squares

225 ml/8 fl oz double cream

2 tbsp rum

holly, to decorate

icing sugar, for dusting

Preheat the oven to 190°C/375°F/Gas Mark 5. Grease with butter and line a 40 x 28-cm/16 x 11-inch Swiss roll tin, then dust with flour.

Reserve 2 tablespoons of the caster sugar and whisk the remainder with the egg yolks in a bowl until thick and pale. Stir in the almond extract. Whisk the egg whites in a separate grease-free bowl until soft peaks form. Gradually whisk in the reserved sugar until stiff and glossy. Sift half the flour over the egg yolk mixture and fold in, then fold in one quarter of the egg whites. Sift and fold in the remaining flour, followed by the remaining egg whites. Spoon the mixture into the tin, spreading it out evenly with a palette knife. Bake in the preheated oven for 15 minutes, until lightly golden.

Sprinkle caster sugar over a sheet of greaseproof paper and turn out the cake on to the paper. Roll up and leave to cool.

Place the chocolate in a heatproof bowl. Bring the cream to boiling point in a small saucepan, then pour it over the chocolate and stir until the chocolate has melted. Beat with an electric mixer until smooth and thick. Reserve about one third of the chocolate mixture and stir the rum into the remainder. Unroll the cake and spread the chocolate and rum mixture over. Re-roll and place on a plate or silver board. Spread the reserved chocolate mixture evenly over the top and sides. Mark with a fork so that the surface resembles tree bark. Just before serving, decorate with holly and dust with icing sugar to resemble snow.

Chocolate Chestnut Roulade

serves 6

6 large eggs, separated

150 g/5½ oz unrefined caster sugar

½ tsp vanilla or chocolate extract

50 g/1¾ oz cocoa powder

icing sugar, for dusting

250 ml/9 fl oz double cream

250 g/9 oz sweetened chestnut purée

2 tbsp brandy

70 g/2½ oz cooked peeled chestnuts, chopped

Preheat the oven to 180°C/350°F/Gas Mark 4. Line a 23 x 45-cm (9 x 17¾-inch) Swiss roll tin with baking paper.

Using an electric whisk, beat the egg yolks, caster sugar and vanilla extract together in a bowl for 10 minutes, or until doubled in volume and pale and fluffy. In a separate bowl, whisk the egg whites until they form soft peaks. Fold a tablespoonful of egg whites into the egg yolk mixture, then gently fold in the remaining egg whites and the cocoa powder.

Spoon the cake mixture into the prepared tin and smooth the surface with a palette knife. Bake in the preheated oven for 20 minutes until risen. Leave to cool in the tin.

Put a large piece of baking paper over a clean tea towel and dust with icing sugar, invert the sponge on to the baking paper and carefully peel away the lining paper. In a clean bowl, whisk the cream until stiff, then stir in the chestnut purée and the brandy. Spread over the sponge, leaving a 2.5-cm/1-inch margin around the edges, and scatter over the chestnuts. Using one end of the tea towel, carefully roll up the roulade. Dust with more icing sugar.

Roast Plums with Armagnac Fool

serves 6

24 ripe plums

50 g/1¾ oz unsalted butter, plus extra for greasing

2 tbsp maple syrup or flower honey

300 ml/10 fl oz double cream

2 tbsp icing sugar

2 large egg whites

2 tbsp Armagnac or brandy

finely grated rind of 1 lemon

1 tsp rosewater (optional)

Preheat the oven to 200°C/400°F/Gas Mark 6. Grease a baking dish with butter.

Cut each plum in half and remove and discard the stone. Place cut-sides up on the prepared baking dish, dot each plum with some of the butter and drizzle over the maple syrup. Cover with foil. Bake in the preheated oven for 20–25 minutes until tender. Leave to cool.

Whisk the cream in a bowl until beginning to thicken, adding a little sugar at a time. In a separate bowl, whisk the egg whites until stiff. Stir the Armagnac into the cream, then fold in the egg whites, followed by half the lemon rind.

To serve, divide the plum halves among 6 serving plates, drizzle over the rosewater, if using, and serve alongside the fool. Scatter over the remaining lemon rind and serve.

Orange Ice Cream with Almond Praline

serves 6

1 large orange, sliced

100 g/3½ oz white granulated sugar

175 ml/6 fl oz water

½ tsp orange flower water

butter, for greasing

225 g/8 oz unrefined caster sugar

125 g/4½ oz flaked almonds, toasted

ice cream

1 vanilla pod

300 ml/10 fl oz single cream

4 large egg yolks

2 tsp custard powder

50 g/1¾ oz unrefined caster sugar

300 ml/10 fl oz crème fraîche

Cut away the flesh of the orange, leaving the rind and a little pith. Cut the rind into 5-cm/2-inch pieces. Put the granulated sugar and 100 ml/3½ fl oz of the water in a saucepan and heat gently, stirring, until the sugar has dissolved. Bring to the boil and add the orange flower water and orange rind. Reduce the heat and simmer gently for 15–20 minutes. Leave the rind to cool slightly in the syrup, then lift out on to greaseproof paper to cool completely and roughly chop.

Grease a piece of foil with butter. Put the sugar in a saucepan with the remaining water and heat gently, stirring, until the sugar has dissolved. Bring to a simmer, swirling the saucepan, and cook until the syrup reaches a caramel-orange colour. Remove from the heat and tip in the almonds. Stir, pour on to the greased foil and spread out. Leave to cool and harden, then break into shards. To make the ice cream, slit the vanilla pod open and scrape out the seeds. Put the pod and cream in a saucepan and heat gently. Put the vanilla seeds, egg yolks, custard powder and sugar in a heatproof bowl and whisk until smooth. When the cream is about to boil, remove the vanilla pod and, whisking constantly, pour the cream over the egg yolk mixture. Continuing to stir, pour the mixture into the saucepan and bring to the boil. Reduce the heat and simmer until thickened. Plunge the saucepan's base into a bowl of iced water, then stir until cool. Fold in the crème fraîche and orange peel. When cold, pour into a freezerproof container, cover and freeze for 12 hours. Remove from the freezer and beat to break down any ice crystals. Re-freeze and beat as before, then re-freeze until solid. Serve with the praline.

Cheesecake with Caramel Pecan Nuts

serves 6–8

base

50 g/1¾ oz pecan nuts

150 g/5½ oz digestive biscuits, broken into pieces

50 g/1¾ oz salted butter, melted

filling

400 g/14 oz cream cheese

200 g/7 oz curd cheese

125 g/4½ oz unrefined caster sugar

3 large eggs

3 large egg yolks

200 ml/7 fl oz double cream

topping

butter, for greasing

225 g/8 oz unrefined caster sugar

5 tbsp water

70 g/2½ oz pecan nuts

Preheat the oven to 160°C/325°F/Gas Mark 3. To make the base, put the pecan nuts in a food processor and process briefly, then add the broken biscuits and pulse again to form crumbs. Tip into a bowl and stir in the melted butter until well combined. Press this into the base of a 20-cm/8-inch springform cake tin. Bake in the preheated oven for 10 minutes. Leave to cool.

To make the filling, beat the cream cheese, curd cheese and sugar together in a large bowl. Beat in the eggs and egg yolks, one at a time, until smooth. Finally, stir in the cream. Spoon over the prepared base. Bake in the preheated oven for 1 hour, then test – the cheesecake should be cooked but with a slight 'wobble' in the centre. Return to the oven for a further 10 minutes if necessary. Leave to cool in the tin.

To make the topping, grease a piece of foil with butter and lay it flat. Put the sugar and water in a saucepan and heat gently, stirring, until the sugar has dissolved. Bring to a simmer, swirling the saucepan rather than stirring, and cook until the syrup begins to darken to form the caramel, then add the pecan nuts. Lift each pecan nut out on to the greased foil and leave to harden. When you are ready to serve, unmould the cheesecake on to a serving plate and arrange the caramel pecan nuts on top.

Traditional Apple Pie

serves 8

pastry

350 g/12 oz plain flour

pinch of salt

85 g/3 oz butter or margarine, chilled and diced

85 g/3 oz lard or white vegetable fat, chilled and diced

about 6 tbsp cold water

beaten egg or milk, for glazing

filling

750 g–1 kg/1 lb 10 oz–2 lb 4 oz cooking apples, peeled, cored and sliced

125 g/4½ oz soft light brown sugar or caster sugar, plus extra for sprinkling

½–1 tsp ground cinnamon, mixed spice or ground ginger

1–2 tbsp water (optional)

To make the pastry, sift the flour and salt into a bowl. Add the butter and fat and rub in with the fingertips until the mixture resembles fine breadcrumbs. Add the water and gather the mixture together into a dough. Wrap the dough in clingfilm and chill in the refrigerator for 30 minutes.

Preheat the oven to 220°C/425°F/Gas Mark 7. Roll out almost two-thirds of the pastry thinly and use to line a deep 23-cm/9-inch pie plate or pie tin.

To make the filling, mix the apples with the sugar and spice and pack into the pastry case; the filling can come up above the rim. Add the water if needed, particularly if the apples are not very juicy.

Roll out the remaining pastry to form a lid. Dampen the edges of the pie rim with water and position the lid, pressing the edges firmly together. Trim and crimp the edges. Use the trimmings to cut out leaves or other shapes to decorate the top of the pie, dampen with water and attach. Glaze the top of the pie with beaten egg or milk, make 1–2 slits in the top and place the pie on a baking sheet.

Bake in the preheated oven for 20 minutes, then reduce the temperature to 180°C/350°F/Gas Mark 4 and bake for a further 30 minutes, or until the pastry is a light golden brown. Serve hot or cold, sprinkled with sugar.

Festive Mince Pies

serves 16

100 g/3½ oz butter, plus extra for greasing

200 g/7 oz plain flour, plus extra for dusting

25 g/1 oz icing sugar

1 egg yolk

2–3 tbsp milk, plus extra for glazing

300 g/10½ oz mincemeat

icing sugar, for dusting

Preheat the oven to 180°C/350°F/Gas Mark 4. Grease a 16-hole tartlet tin with butter. Sift the flour into a bowl. Using your fingertips, rub in the remaining butter until the mixture resembles breadcrumbs. Stir in the sugar and egg yolk. Stir in enough milk to make a soft dough, turn out on to a lightly floured work surface and knead lightly until smooth.

Shape the dough into a ball and roll out to a thickness of 1 cm/½ inch. Use fluted cutters to cut out 16 rounds measuring 7 cm/2¾ inches in diameter and use to line the holes in the tartlet tin. Half-fill each pie with mincemeat. Cut out 16 star shapes from the leftover dough, brush with milk and place on top of each pie. Glaze the surface with more milk and bake in the preheated oven for 15 minutes until the pastry is a pale golden colour. Remove from the oven and leave to cool on a wire rack. Dust with icing sugar before serving.

Christmas Spiced Loaf

serves 6

450 g/1 lb strong white flour, plus extra for dusting

pinch of salt

2 tsp mixed spice

115 g/4 oz unsalted butter, chilled and diced

7-g/⅙-oz sachet easy-blend dried yeast

115 g/4 oz unrefined caster sugar

115 g/4 oz currants

115 g/4 oz raisins

50 g/1¾ oz mixed peel, chopped

finely grated rind of 1 orange

1 egg, beaten

150 ml/5 fl oz milk, warmed

vegetable oil, for oiling

Sift the flour, salt and mixed spice into a bowl and rub in the butter until the mixture resembles breadcrumbs. Stir in the yeast, sugar, dried fruit, mixed peel and orange rind, then add the egg and the warm milk and bring together to form a soft dough. Knead the dough briefly on a floured work surface. Flour a clean bowl and add the dough. Cover the bowl and leave to rise in a warm place for 2 hours.

Preheat the oven to 180°C/350°F/Gas Mark 4 and oil a 900-g/2-lb loaf tin. Knead the dough again briefly, then place it in the tin, cover and leave to prove for 20 minutes. Bake in the preheated oven for 1 hour 10 minutes – the loaf should be golden and well risen. Leave to cool in the tin.

Dark & White Chocolate Florentines

makes 20

25 g/1 oz unsalted butter, plus extra for greasing

15 g/½ oz plain flour, plus extra for dusting

70 g/2½ oz unrefined caster sugar

4 tbsp double cream

50 g/1¾ oz whole blanched almonds, roughly chopped

50 g/1¾ oz flaked almonds, toasted

50 g/1¾ oz mixed peel, chopped

50 g/1¾ oz undyed glacé cherries, chopped

50 g/1¾ oz preserved stem ginger, drained and chopped

70 g/2½ oz plain chocolate, minimum 70% cocoa solids, broken into pieces

70 g/2½ oz white chocolate, broken into pieces

Preheat the oven to 190°C/375°F/Gas Mark 5. Lightly grease 2 baking sheets with butter and dust with flour, shaking to remove any excess.

Put the remaining butter, sugar and flour in a small saucepan and heat gently, stirring well, until the mixture has melted. Gradually add the cream, stirring constantly, then add all the remaining ingredients, except the chocolate, and stir thoroughly. Remove from the heat and leave to cool.

Drop 5 teaspoonfuls of the mixture on to each of the prepared baking sheets, spaced well apart to allow for spreading, then flatten with the back of a spoon. Bake in the preheated oven for 12–15 minutes. Leave the biscuits to harden on the sheets for 2–3 minutes before transferring to a wire rack. Repeat with the remaining mixture, again using the 2 baking sheets.

When the biscuits are completely cool, put the plain chocolate in a heatproof bowl, set the bowl over a saucepan of barely simmering water and heat until melted. Using a teaspoon, spread the base of 10 of the biscuits with the melted chocolate and place chocolate side-up on a wire rack to set. Repeat with the white chocolate and the remaining 10 biscuits.

Cranberry Muffins

makes 18

butter, for greasing

225 g/8 oz plain flour

2 tsp baking powder

½ tsp salt

50 g/1¾ oz caster sugar

55 g/2 oz unsalted butter, melted

2 eggs, lightly beaten

175 ml/6 fl oz milk

115 g/4 oz fresh cranberries

50 g/1¾ oz Parmesan cheese, freshly grated

Preheat the oven to 200°C/400°F/Gas Mark 6. Lightly grease two 9-cup muffin tins with butter.

Sift the flour, baking powder and salt into a bowl. Stir in the sugar. Combine the butter, eggs and milk in a separate bowl, then pour into the bowl of dry ingredients. Stir until all of the ingredients are evenly combined, then stir in the fresh cranberries.

Divide the mixture evenly between the prepared 18 cups in the muffin tins. Sprinkle the grated Parmesan cheese over the top. Bake in the preheated oven for 20 minutes until risen and golden.

Remove the muffins from the oven and leave to cool slightly in the tins. Put the muffins on a wire rack and leave to cool completely.

Chocolate Truffle Selection

makes 40–50

225 g/8 oz plain chocolate, minimum 70% cocoa solids

175 ml/6 fl oz whipping cream

cocoa powder, icing sugar or chopped toasted almonds, for coating

Roughly chop the chocolate and put in a large heatproof bowl. Put the cream in a saucepan and bring up to boiling point. Pour over the chocolate and whisk until smooth. Leave to cool at room temperature for 1½–2 hours.

Cover 2 baking sheets with clingfilm or baking paper. Using a teaspoon, take bite-sized scoops of the chocolate mixture and roll in cocoa powder, icing sugar or chopped nuts to form balls, then place on the prepared baking sheets and chill in the refrigerator until set.

Christmas Tree Biscuits

makes 12

150 g/5½ oz plain flour, plus extra for dusting

1 tsp ground cinnamon

½ tsp ground nutmeg

½ tsp ground ginger

70 g/2½ oz unsalted butter, diced, plus extra for greasing

3 tbsp honey

white icing (optional) and narrow gold or silver ribbon, to decorate

Sift the flour and spices into a bowl and rub in the butter until the mixture resembles breadcrumbs. Add the honey and mix together well to form a soft dough. Wrap the dough in clingfilm and chill in the refrigerator for 30 minutes.

Meanwhile, preheat the oven to 180°C/350°F/Gas Mark 4 and lightly grease 2 baking sheets with butter. Divide the dough in half. Roll out 1 piece of dough on a floured work surface to about 5 mm/¼ inch thick. Cut out tree shapes using a cutter or cardboard template. Repeat with the remaining piece of dough.

Put the biscuits on the prepared baking sheets and, using a cocktail stick, make a hole through the top of each biscuit large enough to thread the ribbon through. Chill in the refrigerator for 15 minutes.

Bake the biscuits in the preheated oven for 10–12 minutes until golden. Leave to cool on the baking sheets for 5 minutes, then transfer to a wire rack to cool completely. Decorate the trees with white icing, or simply leave them plain, then thread a length of ribbon through each hole and tie a knot. Hang from the Christmas tree.

Christmas Angels

makes about 25

225 g/8 oz butter, softened

140 g/5 oz caster sugar

1 egg yolk, lightly beaten

2 tsp passion fruit pulp

280 g/10 oz plain flour

55 g/2 oz desiccated coconut

salt

edible silver glitter, to decorate

icing

175 g/6 oz icing sugar

1–1½ tbsp passion fruit pulp

Put the butter and sugar into a bowl and mix well with a wooden spoon, then beat in the egg yolk and passion fruit pulp. Sift the flour and a pinch of salt into the mixture, add the coconut and stir until thoroughly combined. Halve the dough, shape into balls, wrap in clingfilm and chill in the refrigerator for 30–60 minutes. Preheat the oven to 190°C/375°F/Gas Mark 5. Line 2 baking sheets with baking parchment.

Unwrap the dough and roll out between 2 sheets of baking parchment. Stamp out cookies with a 7-cm/2¾-inch angel-shaped cutter and put them on the prepared baking sheets spaced well apart.

Bake for 10–15 minutes, until light golden brown. Leave to cool on the baking sheets for 5–10 minutes, then using a palette knife, carefully transfer to wire racks to cool completely.

Sift the icing sugar into a bowl and stir in the passion fruit pulp until the icing has the consistency of thick cream. Leave the cookies on the racks and spread the icing over them. Sprinkle with the edible glitter and leave to set.

Christmas Bells

makes about 30

225 g/8 oz butter, softened

140 g/5 oz caster sugar

finely grated rind
of 1 lemon

1 egg yolk, lightly beaten

280 g/10 oz plain flour

½ tsp ground cinnamon

100 g/3½ oz plain
chocolate chips

salt

30 silver balls and food
colouring pens,
to decorate

icing

2 tbsp lightly beaten egg
white

2 tbsp lemon juice

225 g/8 oz icing sugar

Put the butter, sugar and lemon rind into a bowl and mix well with a wooden spoon, then beat in the egg yolk. Sift the flour, cinnamon and a pinch of salt into the mixture, add the chocolate chips and stir until thoroughly combined. Halve the dough, shape into balls, wrap in clingfilm and chill in the refrigerator for 30–60 minutes.

Preheat the oven to 190°C/375°F/Gas Mark 5. Line 2 baking sheets with baking parchment. Unwrap the dough and roll out between 2 sheets of baking parchment. Stamp out cookies with a 5-cm/2-inch bell-shaped cutter and put them on the prepared baking sheets spaced well apart.

Bake for 10–15 minutes, until light golden brown. Leave to cool on the baking sheets for 5–10 minutes, then using a palette knife, carefully transfer to wire racks to cool completely.

Mix together the egg white and lemon juice in a bowl, then gradually beat in the icing sugar until smooth. Leave the cookies on the racks and spread the icing over them. Place a silver ball on the clapper shape at the bottom of each cookie and leave to set completely. When the icing is dry, use the food colouring pens to draw patterns on the cookies.

Mulled Ale & Mulled Wine

mulled ale

makes 2.8 litres/5 pints

2.5 litres/4½ pints strong ale

300 ml/10 fl oz brandy

2 tbsp caster sugar

large pinch of ground cloves

large pinch of ground ginger

mulled wine

makes 3.3 litres/5¾ pints

5 oranges

50 cloves

thinly pared rind and juice of 4 lemons

850 ml/1½ pints water

115 g/4 oz caster sugar

2 cinnamon sticks

2 litres/3½ pints red wine

150 ml/5 fl oz brandy

Mulled Ale

Put all the ingredients in a heavy-based saucepan and heat gently, stirring, until the sugar has dissolved. Continue to heat so that it is simmering but not boiling. Remove the saucepan from the heat and serve the ale immediately in heatproof glasses.

Mulled Wine

Prick the skins of 3 of the oranges all over with a fork and stud with the cloves, then set aside. Thinly pare the rind and squeeze the juice from the remaining oranges.

Put the orange rind and juice, lemon rind and juice, water, sugar and cinnamon in a heavy-based saucepan and bring to the boil over a medium heat, stirring occasionally, until the sugar has dissolved. Boil for 2 minutes without stirring, then remove from the heat, stir once and leave to stand for 10 minutes. Strain the liquid into a heatproof jug, pressing down on the contents of the sieve to extract all the juice.

Pour the wine into a separate saucepan and add the strained spiced juices, the brandy and the clove-studded oranges. Simmer gently without boiling, then remove the saucepan from the heat. Strain into heatproof glasses and serve immediately.

Hot Rum Punch

serves 4.3 litres/7½ pints

850 ml/1½ pints rum

850 ml/1½ pints brandy

600 ml/1 pint freshly squeezed lemon juice

3–4 tbsp caster sugar

2 litres/3½ pints boiling water

slices of fruit, to decorate

Mix together the rum, brandy, lemon juice and 3 tablespoons of the sugar in a punch bowl or large heatproof mixing bowl. Pour in the boiling water and stir well to mix. Taste and add more sugar if required. Decorate with the fruit slices and serve immediately in heatproof glasses with handles.